RAREBIT COOKING SIX

RAREBIT COOKING SIX

CAROLINE MACLEOD

Library of Congress Control Number:		2021903919
ISBN:	Hardcover	978-1-6641-1501-9
	Softcover	978-1-6641-1500-2
	eBook	978-1-6641-1499-9

Print information available on the last page.

Rev. date: 02/24/2021

To order additional copies of this book, contact:
Xlibris
UK TFN: 0800 0148620 (Toll Free inside the UK)
UK Local: 02036 956328 (+44 20 3695 6328 from outside the UK)
www.Xlibrispublishing.co.uk
Orders@Xlibrispublishing.co.uk
824687

CONTENTS

SOLDIERS SIX FIGHTING

INTRODUCTION

This is the second book of two, the first being *To Loose All Plums*. Written in a conversational style, this book provides an easy way to cook simply and is filled with many straightforward tips and hints.

We live in a world that cares more about money than health in eating. We have become so worried about our weight that we are becoming scared of walking around. We all struggle to cope, so occasionally, eating a little bit of what we fancy does us good.

SECTION 1

HAM

1 gammon joint
water
1 bay leaf
peppercorns
cloves
Dijon mustard
demerara sugar

Soak the gammon in water overnight in the fridge and then discard the water.

Place the ham in a pan. Add the peppercorns and enough water to cover ham. Bring to a gentle simmer and continue to simmer for 1 1/2 hours. Cool in the water.

Remove the ham from the pan and slice off the skin, leaving all the white fat underneath the skin on the ham.

Crisscross the meat in a diamond pattern on the fat and put a clove in each diamond. Spread the Dijon mustard over the fat, and sprinkle the sugar over it, patting it down on the sides. Leave the meat bare.

Bake in the oven at 220 degrees C for 12–15 minutes or until a crust is formed.

MARZIPAN

apricot glaze
cake
marzipan/almond paste
icing

Warm the apricot glaze and spread on to the cake. Roll out the marzipan to a 1/2 centimetre thickness, and cover the top of the cake. Let rest uncovered at room temperature for 2 hours; then top with icing.

WHITE ROYAL GLAZE ICING

1 egg white
1 teaspoon glycerine
1 teaspoon rose water
1 kilogram of icing sugar

Combine egg white, glycerine, and rose water into a mixing bowl. Gradually add icing sugar until the mixture is very stiff and too hard to mix. Spoon onto cake, and roughly fork it to make a snow scene.

MINCE PIES

2 packets of ready-rolled shortcrust pastry
2 fluid ounces of rum
1 good bottle of mincemeat
1 egg, beaten
2 ounces caster sugar

Roll out the pastry to 1/2 centimetre thickness. Add the rum to the mincemeat. Make up the mince pies. Don't put in too much filling. (That way, you can eat more of them.)

Seal and cover with egg wash and a sprinkling of sugar.

Bake at 220 degrees C for 15–20 minutes.

RUM TRIFLE

10 ounces granulated sugar
3/4 pint water
2 packets of trifle cakes or sponge fingers
1/2 bottle of rum
1/2 pint freshly squeezed orange juice
2 cartons of strawberries or frozen raspberries, sliced (set aside a few for decoration)
custard
cream
flaked chocolate

Make simple syrup by boiling granulated sugar in water for 8 minutes.

Put trifle cakes in bottom of pudding basin and top with syrup, rum, orange juice, and strawberries or raspberries.

Pour over custard and leave for a couple of hours.

Whisk cream until soft, thick peaks form. Place on top of custard.

Decorate with flaked chocolate and remaining fruit.

CHOCOLATE FUDGE CHEESECAKE

1 packet of toffee
1 pint of double cream
3/4 pack of butter
200 grammes dark chocolate
1 packet cream cheese
4 eggs
6 ounces self-raising flour
pastry case, baked

Melt together the toffee, cream, butter, and dark chocolate on medium heat, or put in the microwave on high, 1 minute at a time, until the chocolate has melted.

Mix cream cheese, eggs, and self-raising flour; add toffee/chocolate mixture.

Pour into pastry case, and bake in the oven at 150 degrees C for 45 minutes or until set in the centre.

FRIED STEAK WITH MUSHROOM SAUCE

flour
salt and pepper
1/2 inch thick rump steak
oil
wild porcini mushrooms
10 fluid ounces beef stock
1/2 pint cream
baked potatoes and broccoli

Put the flour onto a plate and add a generous amount of salt and pepper.

Rub the steak into flour mixture.

Fry on a griddle with a little hot oil on high heat for 3 minutes on each side, turning frequently. Reduce to medium heat and fry a further 3 minutes on each side.

Put the mushrooms into 10 fluid ounces of beef stock and bring to a boil for 5 minutes. Add cream, and boil for 10 minutes to reduce the sauce. Add salt and pepper to taste

Serve with baked potatoes and broccoli.

TURKEY FRICASSEE

white meat turkey
dark meat turkey
barbecue sauce
white sauce
mashed potatoes and sweet corn

Mix barbecue sauce with the dark meat, and bake in the oven at 200 degrees C for 20–25 minutes.

Make a white sauce and cook the white meat in it for several minutes.

Serve with mashed potatoes and sweet corn.

SCRAMBLED EGGS

Serves 1

butter
salt and pepper, to taste
2–3 eggs
hot buttered toast

Melt butter in a saucepan. Add salt and pepper. Heat until butter is foaming.

Crack in the eggs. Mix with a wooden spoon quite quickly over a brisk heat until soft.

Take off heat, and serve immediately with hot buttered toast.

DROP SCONES

1 egg
2 1/2 ounces plain flour
1 ounce granulated white sugar
a handful of sultanas
5 fluid ounces of sour cream
1 teaspoon of baking powder
milk
butter
vegetable oil
strawberry jam

Mix first seven ingredients together, and beat with a whisk until creamy. The mixture should hold to the back of a spoon that is dipped into it.

Heat a little butter and vegetable oil in a frying pan. When it is sizzling, add teaspoonfuls of the mixture separately into the pan. Cook until brown on both sides.

Enjoy while still warm; spread with butter and strawberry jam.

MERINGUE ROLL

eggs
double cream
1 tablespoon Grand Marnier
icing sugar, divided
raspberries

Make a meringue, and put it in a large Swiss roll tin or on a large flat baking sheet with a nonstick silicone baking paper. Cook at 150 degrees C for 50 minutes. Cool completely.

Combine cream, Grand Marnier, and 1 tablespoon icing suger. Whip and spread on meringue; then top with raspberries.

Roll meringue using the silicone paper, scraping the meringue back from the paper as you roll it.

Dust with remaining icing sugar.

ASPARAGUS WITH HOLLANDAISE SAUCE

asparagus
water
salt
pre-prepared hollandaise sauce

Cut off the woody ends from the asparagus stalks—usually only 1 inch (3 centimetres) or so from the shop-bought ones. Leave the bumpy tips to eat; they are the best bit.

Bring a pan of salted water to a boil. Add aspargus and boil for 7 minutes or until the main stalk is tender and can be cut with a table knife.

Top with warmed hollandaise sauce.

HALIBUT WITH ONION SAUCE

Serves 2

1 large white onion, sliced
vegetable oil
seasoning
1 teaspoon sugar
1/2 pint double cream
chopped parsley
lemon juice
2 thick halibut steaks
peas and new potatoes

Sauté onion in vegetable oil on medium heat until clear and soft. Add seasoning and sugar, and cook for a few minutes until carmelized. Add double cream, chopped parsley, and a drop of lemon juice, and warm through.

Fry the halibut on both sides on gentle to medium heat for about 6 minutes, each side. (If you are not sure whether it is cooked through, take a table knife and cut some aside to be certain.)

Top with the cream sauce.

Serve with buttered and seasoned peas and new potatoes, cooked without salt and seasoned with melted butter, salt, and pepper.

APPLE FOOL

2 cooking apples, peeled, cored, and chopped
150 grammes granulated white sugar
1 pint double cream

Cook apples with white sugar and a drop of water in a covered pan over high heat, until pureed. Set aside to cool.

Whip double cream until it is stiff and falls off the back of a spoon with the flick of a hand.

Gently fold in apple puree, 2 tablespoons at a time, so as not to loosen the cream too much. Fool should be thick.

ARMENIAN LAMB

1/2 shoulder of lamb
1 large white onion, sliced
vegetable oil
1 tablespoon sugar
flour
salt
pepper
juice of one fresh orange
1 can chopped tomatoes
1 can chickpeas, rinsed and drained
water
mashed potatoes

Chop shoulder of lamb into 2-inch pieces, leaving on the fat and removing the bone.

Cook onion in vegetable oil in a casserole dish or pan on top of stove. Add sugar and caramelize for a few more seconds.

Coat lamb with flour, salt, and pepper. Add to the onion on medium heat, adding a touch more vegetable oil, if necessary. Add orange juice, tomatoes, and chickpeas. Cover the meat in the pan with water.

Put in the oven at 180 degrees C for 2 1/2 hours.

Serve with mashed potatoes.

RHUBARB SPONGE

2 cans rhubarb, one drained of syrup
half a small packet of brown sugar
250 grammes butter
200 grammes self-raising flour
custard

Put rhubarb in a pie dish.

In a separate bowl, combine brown sugar, butter, and flour. Crumble until the mixture looks like bread crumbs (as if it could turn into pastry at any second). Spread on top of rhubarb, and bake in the oven at 180 degrees C for 45 minutes or until the top is golden brown.

Serve with custard.

BEEF WITH ASPARAGUS

4 ounces of fillet steak
asparagus
butter
light olive oil
black pepper
lemon juice
salt
mixed salad

Cut steak into very thin strips (so that you can nearly see through them).

Cut woody ends off aparagus stalks, leaving about 3-inch stalks, including the tips. Steam them for 10 minutes.

Fry the fillet steak on a griddle over very hot heat, burning them slightly. Place steak and asparagus on a plate of mixed salad.

Melt butter and mix with light olive oil, black pepper, and lemon juice. Add some salt. Pour over the asparagus and fillet steak, and serve with mixed salad.

POTATO PIE

potatoes, cut into thick chunks
butter
pastry (for top and bottom crusts)
strong cheese
1/4 pint double cream
egg yolk
salt

Boil potatoes for 5 minutes; then fry in butter.

Line a flan dish with bottom pastry. Place cheese on the pastry. Pile on the potatoes, and add more cheese. Pour double cream over all; then cover with top pastry.

Brush top with egg yolk and salt, and bake at 200 degrees C until the pastry is cooked (about 40 minutes).

SECTION 2

BEEF STEW WITH CARAMELIZED ONIONS AND SAUTÉED MUSHROOMS

braising steak, cut into large cubes
flour
salt and pepper
carrots, cut into large pieces
button onions, chopped
vegetable oil
water
butter
mushrooms
sugar
mashed potatoes

Dredge steak cubes with flour, salt, and pepper. Sauté carrots and most of the onions in vegetable oil in a deep pan. (Set some onions aside.) Then add steak pieces and more vegetable oil. Fry on medium to high heat until brown. Add water to just cover the meat and cook at 180 degrees C for 3 1/2 hours, or cook on the top of the hob. Stir frequently.

While stew is cooking, cook reserved onions and mushrooms in butter; then further cook with sugar for a few minutes to caramelize them.

Add the caramelized onions and mushrooms just before serving. Allow the mushrooms and onions to heat through in the stew.

Serve with mashed potatoes.

APPLE CRUMBLE

Cooked Apples

4 cooking apples
4 tablespoons granulated sugar
water
cinnamon (optional)

Crumble

200 grammes plain flour
150 grammes sugar
1 packet (250 grammes) butter (hard, not softened)

custard

Peel, core, and slice apples. Place in ovenproof bowl with 4 tablespoons of sugar and a little water. Add a sprinkling of cinnamon, if you like it.

To make the crumble, mix flour and sugar. Work hard butter into the flour and sugar mixture with your fingers or a knife.

When it resembles sticky bread crumbs, spread it on top of the apples and cook for 45 minutes at 170 degrees C, or until the topping has turned dark golden brown.

Serve with custard.

QUEEN'S PUDDING

Custard

6 eggs, separated
2 teaspoons cornflour
12 ounces caster sugar, divided in half
1 pint cream
2 fluid ounces Cointreau or other orange-flavoured liqueur

Filling

peaches, pitted and halved
handful of hazelnuts

To make custard, thoroughly mix egg yolks with cornflour in a medium bowl.

Blend 6 ounces caster sugar into cream in a saucepan, and heat until warm. Add Cointreau, then pour onto the egg yolks, mixing quickly. Return to the saucepan. Over gentle heat, bring to just below simmering point.

Place halved peaches in a pudding dish. Pour the custard on top of the halved peaches. Scatter hazelnuts over the peaches and custard.

Set the custard in a bain-marie (a deep pan filled with water to one-third the height of the pudding dish), and bake in an oven at 170 degrees C for 40 minutes.

While it is baking, beat the egg whites in a small pan until firm, and add remaining 6 ounces of caster sugar. Heat until the mixture is glossy.

When cook time is finished for the bain-marie, put egg whites on top of the peaches and custard. Bake for another 35 minutes in the bain-marie.

CRÈME ANGLAISE TART WITH STRAWBERRIES AND RED GLAZE

1 pint milk, plus one drop
4 egg yolks
vanilla essence
5 ounces granulated sugar
Plain flour
1 dessertspoon (10 ml) plain flour
1/2 pint double cream
1 packet of shortcrust pastry
1 packet of strawberries, washed and cut into small pieces
strawberry glaze (from supermarket)

Heat milk until warm.

Put egg yolks in a saucepan with a few drops of vanilla essence, 5 ounces of granulated sugar, and 1 dessertspoon of plain flour. Mix together with a drop of cool milk.

Pour the warm milk into the egg yolks while mixing quickly (so the yolks dissipate and curdle). Heat to just below simmering point, and then immediately take off the heat (otherwise, the eggs will cook).

Let cool, stirring for a little while to make sure the custard doesn't catch on the bottom of the pan. (Do not overstir, or the custard will go runny again.)

When the custard is cold, whip the double cream in a bowl and fold it into the custard.

Meanwhile, roll out a packet of shortcrust pastry and line some small tins. Put a greaseproof lining on top of each pastry and fill with dried beans before baking. (This is baking "blind".) Bake at 200 degrees C for 20 minutes.

When the pastry is cool, fill it with the crème anglaise and scatter strawberries on top. Cover with the strawberry glaze, and serve.

ROASTED RED PEPPERS

red peppers
fennel, chopped
buffalo mozzarella, cut into thick slices
rehydrated wild mushrooms
olive oil
garlic cloves, chopped
salt and pepper
french bread

Cut red peppers in half through the middle and pop into a roasting tin with chopped fennel, buffalo mozzarella slices, and rehydrated wild mushrooms.

Sprinkle with olive oil, garlic, salt, and pepper.

Bake at 200 degrees C for 45 minutes.

Serve with french bread.

PAELLA WITH PANCETTA

risotto rice
1 onion, chopped
olive oil
2 red chilli peppers, chopped, with seeds
water
ham stock
rehydrated wild mushrooms
panchetta
peas
goat's cheese
fresh marjoram
salt and pepper
green salad

Put risotto rice in a pan with the chopped onion, olive oil, and chilli peppers and seeds.

In a separate pan, boil water.

Fry the rice mixture for 3 minutes; then add some boiling water and some ham stock.

Rehydrate wild mushrooms according to the packet instructions; then add to rice mixture and cook until the water has been absorbed, adding more water until the rice is cooked al dente and is still soupy.

Add the pancetta, peas, goat's cheese, and some fresh marjor am. Season with salt and pepper.

Serve with green salad.

RASPBERRY PHYLLO PASTRY WITH CREAM AND CUSTARD SAUCE

Serves 4

1 packet phyllo pastry
butter, melted
1 pint of double cream
1 ounce of icing sugar, plus extra for sprinkling
1 shot of Grand Marnier
premade custard (from supermarket)
raspberries
caster sugar

Remove 4 sheets phyllo pastry from packet and place one on top of the other, with melted butter brushed all over each sheet. Put melted butter all over the top sheet too.

Make holes with a sharp fork all over the phyllo pastry, and then take a small tart cutter, about 3 inches across, and cut out 12 rounds.

Bake them in the oven at 200 degrees C for about 15 minutes. Let cool.

Whip double cream with icing sugar and Grand Marnier.

Put a dot of cream on the pudding plate for each person; then place a round of baked pastry on the cream.

Place a dessertspoon of cream and a few raspberries on the pastry round. (You can use frozen raspberries if you prefer, but make sure you sweeten them with a little caster sugar, and warm them for several seconds to dissolve the sugar.)

Place a small spoonful of custard on top of the raspberries, and place a pastry piece on top of that. Once you have made them all, sprinkle each with icing sugar—it doesn't matter if some goes on the plate—and serve.

CHICKEN WITH CURRIED CREAM AND SULTANAS

1 chicken breast per person
vegetable oil
2 onions, chopped
1 tablespoon hot Madras curry paste
2 handfuls sultanas
1 pint double pouring cream
1 banana, roughly chopped (optional)
chips

Heat vegetable oil in a deep frying pan and add the chicken breasts (chopped, if you prefer). Cook them over a gentle to medium heat until they are half cooked.

Add chopped onions and hot Madras curry paste, and continue cooking for two minutes until the curry paste has cooked through.

Add sultanas and double pouring cream.

Add the banana, if you like.

Allow the sauce to cook on gentle heat until the cream has dissolved into the sauce and the chicken is firmly cooked.

Serve with chips.

HAM AND YELLOW SPLIT PEA SOUP WITH POTATOES DAUPHINOISE

Soup

2 onions, chopped
2 carrots, chopped
1 leek, chopped
1 swede/turnip, chopped
1 potato, chopped
2 handfuls of yellow split peas
black peppercorns
vegetable oil
3 pints water
1 ham joint

Place onions, carrots, leek, turnip, potato, yellow split peas, and some black peppercorns in a pan, and cook in oil until they have softened slightly.

Add 3 pints of water and the ham joint; bring to a boil. Cook until the peas have totally cooked down.

Take out the ham, and serve after the soup with potatoes dauphinoise.

Potatoes Dauphinoise

potatoes, sliced
half-fat crème fraiche
mustard
salt and pepper, to taste

Mix potatoes, crème fraiche, and mustard in a baking dish. Season with salt and pepper. Cook the potatoes at 200 degrees C for 1 hour.

ROAST VENISON

4/5 pound joint of venison
salt and pepper
oil
1 pint lamb stock
cauliflower cheese, red currant jelly, roast potatoes, and gravy

Put the venison joint in a roasting tin and season with salt and pepper. Add lamb stock.

Cover the joint with silver foil and tighten to the sides of the roasting tin.

Roast the venison for 2 hours at 220 degrees C. (With the bone, the joint will take an extra half hour.)

Serve with cauliflower cheese, red currant jelly, and roast potatoes and gravy.

HOLLANDAISE

8 black peppercorns
2 fluid ounces of white wine vinegar
1 teaspoon cumin
6 egg yolks
salt, to taste
2 packets of butter, softened

Put peppercorns, vinegar, and cumin in a double saucepan and boil rapidly for 1 minute.

Take the top saucepan off the bottom saucepan, and let the remaining liquid cool slightly; let the top pan go cool, but leave bottom pan on the heat.

Add all of the egg yolks at once, into top saucepan, along with a bit of the softened butter, whisking continuously. Return the saucepan to the bottom saucepan on the heat. The water in the double saucepan should be simmering rapidly. Continue rapidly adding the pieces of butter to the mixture whilst still whisking rapidly. The mixture should start to thicken.

Continue to add all the butter in bits, whisking continuously. Take the saucepan off the heat immediately when the sauce has thickened. Do not reheat.

Don't worry if it is a bit runny; it will still taste nice.

Be careful not to let the sauce in the top saucepan get too hot or it will cook the egg yolks and curdle.

For bearnaise sauce, just add some tarragon in the butter stage.

"RED" VEAL ESCALOPES

escalopes of veal (I always use calves that have been
fed in the field for approximately one year.)
flour
salt and pepper, to taste
asparagus and hollandaise sauce

Dredge escalopes in flour, salt, and pepper, and fry for 3 minutes on both sides on a medium heat. Cook one after the other.

Serve with asparagus, steamed for 8 minutes, with hollandaise on the side.

PUNCH

3 bottles white wine
1 bottle rosé (cheap sweet sparkling wine)
lots of fruit to eat

Mix wines together. Place fruit in flat glasses; then pour wine on top.

Make sure the glasses are full of fruit and that you have spoons to eat it with.

SQUASH SALAD

squashes, warm, fried, boiled
asparagus
tomatoes
olives
marjoram
mozarella cheese, shredded
olive oil
balsamic vinegar
1 lemon, peeled and separated into segments

Chop first five ingredients to look attractive. Sprinkle with cheese, and drizzle with olive oil and balsamic vinegar. Add lemon segments to the salad at the last minute.

SMOKED SALMON AND GREEN PEA PASTA

chillies, chopped fine
shallots, chopped fine
smoked salmon, torn in pieces
chives, chopped
olive oil
pasta shells, cooked and cold
green peas, cooked and warm
salt and pepper, to taste

Mix everything together and let it rest for an hour. Season with pepper
and a little salt.

"RED" VEAL MINCE WITH PASTA

macaroni, cooked
meat sauce
capers
lemons
tomatoes
pinch of brown sugar or a spoon of treacle
ouzo/pastis
chives
cheese and egg sauce (with ricotta and marscapone)

Layer macaroni with meat sauce, capers, lemons, tomatoes, brown sugar
or treacle, ouzo/pastis, and chives.

Layer cheese and egg sauce, one layer in middle and one layer on top.

PASTA WITH WHITE FISH SAUCE

fish stock
1/2 pint single cream
peas
pinch coriander leaves
pinch flat-leaf parsley
spaghetti/vermicelli, cooked
1/2 lemon, gently squeezed
salt and pepper, to taste
mozarella, grated

Boil together the fish stock and the cream.

Cook peas separately; then add to the sauce.

Add coriander and parsley.

Add pasta and the lemon to the sauce, and mix well.

Season to taste, and serve with the mozarella.

CHICKEN AND WHITEBAIT SALAD

chicken breasts, cut thin
olive oil
whitebait
flour
garlic, chopped
red chilli, chopped
lettuce (romaine) salad
1 lemon, lightly squeezed
salt and pepper, to taste

Fry chicken breasts in olive oil.

Coat whitebait with flour, and fry in oil.

Add chopped garlic and chilli to crisp green salad. Add chicken and whitebait. Drizzle with lemon juice, season with salt and pepper, and serve.

SALMON STICKS

1 salmon fillet, cut into thin strips
olive oil
salt and pepper
savarin moulded rice
turmeric
shallots, chopped

Fry salmon strips on high heat in olive oil, salt, and pepper.

Place over a savarin moulded rice, which has been fried with tumeric and chopped shallots before boiling. Season.

Serve tepid.

ICE CREAM AND TOFFEE SURPRISE

Vanilla Soft Scoop

custard
2 teaspoons of vanilla essence
1 pint of double cream

Mix ingredients together and freeze.

Toffee Mixture

1 packet of toffee
1 can of condensed milk
maple syrup

Melt together toffee with condensed milk. Add some maple syrup. Freeze until stiff, about 2/3 hours.

When vanilla soft scoop and toffee mixture are frozen, loosley fold together, and serve.

ROCK CAKES

1 ounce of dessicated coconut
1 teaspoon almond essence
1 once of plain flour
1 ounce of ground almonds
2 ounces of granulated sugar
1 ounce of currants
5 ounces of butter
water

Mix together all ingredients except butter and water. Then rub in butter and add some water to combine.

Form into rock peaks and bake at 180 degrees C for 14 minutes.

They should look like lava rocks—I was told that in my childhood.

SOLDIERS SIX FIGHTING

For *le repas* and dinner parties

To have a few of your favourite digestives at the end or the beginning of your meal is good.

MENU 1

Toasted Goat's Cheese
Beef Wellington
Raspberry Meringue

Toasted Goat's Cheese

individual goat's cheese
basil
lemon
thyme
oregano
black pepper
1 tablespoon olive oil
crispy green salad and crusty bread

Cut the goat's cheese in half horizontally. Sprinkle herbs and black pepper on the cut side of the goat's cheese.

Drizzle cheese with olive oil, and grill under a moderate to hot grill for 8 minutes or until golden brown.

Serve with crispy green salad and crusty bread.

Beef Wellington

fat-end fillet of beef
salt and pepper
mushroom pate
2 packets of puff pastry
egg, beaten, with salt
new potatoes, carrots, spring cabbage
butter with salt
beurre noisette (gravy)

Season fillet of beef with salt and pepper. Brown on all sides on a hot griddle, and let cool for 5 minutes.

Spread mushroom pate all over the fillet.

Roll out puff pastry to a half-centimetre thickness.

Get the beaten egg with salt ready.

Put the beef in the centre of the rolled-out pastry, and bring the sides up to the top, completely encasing the fillet in pastry. (It might be easier to make the join underneath the fillet.)

Decorate with the leftover pastry by making flowers and sticking them on top of the pastry-encased fillet with some of the beaten egg.

Glaze the whole pastry with beaten egg, and roast in the oven at 220 degrees C for 45 minutes.

Cut in thick slices. Serve with new potatoes, carrots, and spring cabbage (tossed in butter with salt) and gravy.

You may need to add a tablespoon of oil with the butter before browning.

Beurre Noisette

This is the gravy that goes with a beef Wellington. When making beurre noisette, you have to be very quick in the initial stages.

butter
oil (any type)
flour
tomato puree
stock

Brown some butter and oil (some people use walnut oil).

As soon as it starts to go brown and nutty, add some flour and tomato puree.

Then add stock (your favourite type, even fish stock) and whisk it to simmering point for a minute.

Season with salt and pepper.

Raspberry Meringue

Wipe out a mixing bowl and beaters with vinegar to cleanse the grease. Egg whites are particularly prone to underdeveloping when whisked, even when the pots used are clean.

4 eggs, room temperature
6 ounces caster sugar
1 pint double cream
icing sugar
1 fluid ounce Grand Marnier
raspberries
mint leaves

Whisk egg whites with an electric beater or hand whisk until the whites form peaks.

Add a little sugar at a time until it is all used. Keep whisking until the egg whites and sugar are shiny and well thickened into peaks.

Pile the meringue onto baking parchment in a thick circle, and bake at 180 degrees C for 30–40 minutes.

Let cool.

Remove from baking parchment. (You may need to use two pallet knives.)

Whip double cream with a little icing sugar and Grand Marnier until soft and fluffy and forming peaks.

Spread on top of meringue; cover with raspberries and decorate with mint leaves.

MENU 2

Roasted Peppers
Lemon Sole
Chocolate Mousse

Roasted Peppers

red peppers
olive oil
sprats
salt and pepper
crusty bread

Cut a red pepper in half through the green stalk, keeping half the stalk on each side. Use half a stalk for each person.

Place in a roasting pan, cut side up, and drizzle with olive oil.

Place small sprats over the top, and season with salt and pepper.

Roast at 200 degrees C for about 40 minutes.

It will make quite a lot of juices, whichshould be served with the peppers and mopped up with crusty bread.

Lemon Sole

fillet of sole (1 per person)
flour
vegetable oil
salt and pepper
new potatoes and green beans
garlic butter

Dip fillet of sole in flour. Fry quickly in vegetable oil in a frying pan, and season with salt and pepper.

Serve with new potatoes and green beans, coated in garlic butter.

Chocolate Mousse

1/2 pint double cream
200 grammes of chocolate
3 egg whites

Whisk double cream until soft peaks form.

Melt chocolate in the microwave on full power for 1 minute.

Whisk egg whites; then fold all the ingredients together.

Chill.

MENU 3

Eggs Florentine
Trout in Ham and Cream Sauce
Strawberry and Cream Mille Feuille

Eggs Florentine

frozen spinach
nutmeg
salt and pepper
double cream
egg
Parmesan cheese
bread and butter

Put spinach in a saucepan with some butter, and cook it over medium heat until it is all thawed. It will dry out as it cooks.

Add a grating of nutmeg and some salt and pepper.

Put a layer of spinach in a ramekin dish, and add a layer of double cream and then an egg. Sprinkle Parmesan cheese on top.

Bake at 180 degrees C for 15–20 minutes.

Serve with bread and butter.

Trout in Ham and Cream Sauce

1 fillet of trout per person
butter
salt and pepper
parsley, chopped
1/2 pint double cream
ham, sliced thick and then cut into matchsticks
rice and peas

Fry trout in butter, salt and pepper, and chopped parsley for 1 minute on each side.

Pour in double cream. Add ham and simmer for 1 minute.

Serve with rice and peas.

Strawberry and Cream Mille Feuille

1 packet puff pastry
egg yolk
caster sugar
1 ounce icing sugar, plus additional for dusting
1/2 pint double cream
strawberries, chopped

Roll out puff pastry into an oblong shape. Cut 8 oblongs out of it. The pastry should be a 1/2 centimetre thick.

Prick 4 of them all over with a fork. The other 4 should be glazed with egg yolk and sprinkled with caster sugar.

Cook all of the pastry slices at 200 degrees C for 15 minutes or until golden brown.

Take out of the oven and let cool completely.

Whisk icing sugar with double cream until it holds its weight well enough on a spoon.

Add some sugar to strawberries, and leave to macerate for a while.

Fold the strawberries into the cream, leaving a bit of cream for holding down the pastries to the serving plate.

Place the pricked pastry slices on a serving plate, putting a dot of cream underneath each one of them to hold them steady. Place the filling on top of them all, followed by the glazed pastry slices.

Dust them all with icing sugar and serve.

MENU 4

Sea Bream
Bombe Galore

Sea Bream

sea bream fillets (take care to check for bones)
1 pint of double cream
few sprigs of rosemary and basil
salt and pepper
cherry tomatoes
olive oil
linguini, cooked

Simmer double cream with a few sprigs of rosemary and basil and salt and pepper.

Fry the sea bream fillets for 4–5 minutes on each side; then add cream to frying pan and let it heat through.

Meanwhile, roast cherry tomatoes in olive oil, salt, and pepper at 220 degrees C for 20 minutes; then toss with linguini.

Serve sea bream with linguini and cherry tomatoes

Bombe Galore

apricot compote
1 tub of cream cheese
1/2 pint double cream
1 shot rum
4 meringue nests, broken up
fruit

Mix the cream cheese with the double cream.

Carefully fold in the rum, apricot compote, and meringue nests. Put in a pudding bowl and freeze overnight.

Dip in hot water to turn out; decorate with fruit and serve.

MENU 5

Mussels Florentine
Lemon Cream

Mussels Florentine

frozen spinach
butter
salt and pepper
white wine
mussels
cheese sauce
Paremsan cheese, grated

Defrost the spinach in a pan over medium heat with butter, salt, and pepper, stirring regularly.

Put some white wine in a pan with a tight-fitting lid, and add some mussels that have had all of their hair pulled out. Put on high heat and leave to steam for 2–3 minutes after the steam has started to escape from the pan.

Make a cheese sauce.

When the mussels have opened in the pan, remove from the heat straightaway, and remove mussels from the pan. Take the mussels out of the shells, and take care to keep the shells.

Put the shell halves on a baking sheet and fill with spinach; then place a mussel on top, and then top with cheese sauce.

Sprinkle with Parmesan, and place under the grill to brown.

Lemon Cream

1 pint of double cream
rum
2 egg whites
2 ounces of caster sugar
2 lemons

Whip the double cream with the rum.

Whisk the egg whites until they have formed stiff peaks. Add the sugar to the egg whites once they have peaked, and continuing to whisk.

Squeeze the juice out of the lemons and add to the egg whites; then fold in the double cream and rum mixture.

MENU 6

Cheese Souffle
Sea Bass on Red Cabbage

Cheese Souffle

1 pint of very strong-flavoured cheese sauce
3 eggs, separated
crusty bread and butter

Make a pint of very strong-flavoured cheese sauce, and add to it the egg yolks while it is not too hot; beat it in.

Whisk the egg whites until stiff, and fold into the cheese sauce.

Put into a souffle dish until halfway up the sides. Bake in oven at 220 degrees C for 40 minutes.

Serve with crusty bread and butter for dipping.

Sea Bass on Red Cabbage

red cabbage
1 fillet of sea bass per person
white wine
cream fraiche
peppercorns
peas and new potatoes
butter, salt and pepper, and garlic

Make a favourite red cabbage recipe or use red cabbage already made up from a supermarket.

Put the fillets of sea bass in individual silver foil parcels. Add some white wine and crème fraiche and a few peppercorns in each one.

Bake in the oven in a roasting tin at 220 degrees C for 30 minutes.

Serve with peas and new potatoes turned in butter, salt and pepper, and garlic.

MENU 7

Watercress, Beetroot, and Broccoli Salad
Salmon and Plaice Roll
Fresh Fruit Brandy

Watercress, Beetroot, and Broccoli Salad

watercress
broccoli, cut up into tiny florets
fresh beetroot
1/2 cup of olive oil
1 orange, juiced
1 garlic clove, crushed
1 dessertspoon honey
1/2 of 1 chilli
salt and pepper

Thoroughly wash some watercress.

Cook the broccoli florets until just al dente.

Tear the stalks of beetroot; then boil beetroot for 1 1/2 hours or until tender. Remove the skin using rubber gloves to avoid getting reddened fingers; just rub off the skin. Cut beetroot into shreds.

Put olive oil, orange juice, garlic, honey, and chilli into a food processor and mix for 1 minute. Season with salt and pepper.

Put the salad together, and then pour on the dressing and thoroughly mix.

Salmon and Plaice Roll

salmon slices
plaice fillets
1 cup water
1 pint double cream
3 teaspoons Dijon mustard
homemade chips and peas

Roll salmon slices and plaice fillets together on a diagonal, securing them with a toothpick. Place in a roasting dish with the water. Cover them with tin foil and bake them in the oven for 20 minutes at 200 degrees C.

Pour double cream into a frying pan, and add the Dijon mustard. Reduce for 5 minutes; then season to taste.

Serve with homemade chips and peas.

Fresh Fruit Brandy

unsulphured apricots
water
brandy
cream

Place some unsulphured apricots in a saucepan with some water and brandy; bring to simmering point for 20 minutes.

Let cool, and then serve with cream.

Lightning Source UK Ltd.
Milton Keynes UK
UKHW011824110321
380191UK00002B/11/J